LEAD BY ENGAGEMENT

Leaders Must Be Engaged With Their Employees Before Expecting Their Employees To Be Engaged With Their Work

By Moaz Sharif, MBA

Lead By Engagement

Copyright © 2018 by Moaz Sharif, MBA
All rights reserved. Published in 2018
Printed in the United States of America

No part of this book may be reproduced or transmitted in any form or by any means without the written permission of the publisher, except in the case of brief quotations.

ISBN-13: 978-1719183109
ISBN-10: 1719183104

Layout/Cover/ Edits by: solfire@phoenix-farm.com

Lead By Engagement

Table of Contents

INTRODUCTION: 4

NO MORE EXCUSES: IMPROVE YOUR ENGAGEMENT! 8

A BETTER YOU! 20

A FULL PERSON 26

DARE TO DREAM! 34

DREAM KNITTING 48

GAME CHANGER 53

EQ AS A COMPETITIVE BUSINESS ASSET 69

DO YOU KNOW YOURSELF ? PERSONALITY ... 73

INCREASING EMPLOYEE ENGAGEMENT 79

CONCLUSION 86

ABOUT THE AUTHOR 89

INTRODUCTION:

Keeping employees engaged is the biggest challenge for any corporation. A recent Gallup survey revealed that only 13% of employees and managers across the globe are really engaged with their work. Which means that 87% of employees are either disengaged or actively disengaged! That is a huge proportion of any company's workforce.

Disengaged employees and managers just work enough to get by. They don't go beyond what is clearly laid out in their job description, they rarely share ideas that can then benefit the whole team; but the worst effect from this is found in the quality of work produced. This is causing hundreds of billions of dollars in losses to corporations worldwide.

The situation is not much better when looking just in USA. Here, only 26% of employees are engaged leaving 16% of employees in the actively disengaged category that is causing US corporations a loss of $300 billion per year! This doesn't even calculate those 58% of workers in the middle who could do so much better if

Lead By Engagement

they felt more of a connection with their team and their company – the profit increases if you were able to change those masses could be incalculable.

There is no magic formula to convert disengaged employees into engaged employees. However, there *are* ways that this situation can be remedied. Corporations can take steps that will change the working environment and therefore allow more and more employees to become engaged by feeling involved. This book is an effort on my part to sensitize the leaders and managers of our nation's business community to the root causes of the disengagement "epidemic," and I will discuss a number of ways this can be controlled and even reversed.

As a leadership and performance trainer, I have worked with many organizations that were once plagued with this epidemic. The reason that this epidemic creeps in to inflict so many corporations with its low key yet powerful drain on productivity — is the inherent weakness in the will of the organizations and the leaders to fully understand their workers.

Most organizations are so involved with the production, sales, systems and technology which they have to have in place that the people who are the real asset for any corporation are either ignored or are not given first priority. In smaller companies, the owner is often more interested in making profits or serving customers than with the working environment for staff — causing them to forget about the people who actually serve their customers and make money for them.

This disengagement of employees is not because the staff is "bad," it is because their management doesn't know or doesn't care enough about their employees.

Lead By Engagement

A new employee when hired is usually full of enthusiasm and has the will to work and really wants to excel. However, the company environment and poor practices of the management fails to take full advantage of that enthusiasm and, slowly but surely, that wonderful enthusiasm turns into disengagement and sometimes even worse - into active disengagement. An actively disengaged employee is one who feels betrayed and cheated. This employee becomes an enemy within. They are out to get the company. That is why billions of dollars are lost each year.

Disengagement results in many of the following problems:

- Increased turnover
- Low productivity
- Low morale
- High burnout
- High employee conflicts
- Missed deadlines
- Lower quality products/services
- Customer dissatisfaction
- Lack of accountability
- Lo$$e$ to company

In this book I have tried to lay out a guide and explain to you leaders what pitfalls to avoid and the steps you can take to win back your employees. In my experience it is extremely difficult to convert *actively* disengaged employees back to engaged staff. Therefore, the most sensible thing is to focus first on the disengaged employees rather than using your resources on the actively disengaged employees; remember the

Lead By Engagement

ones that are just surviving (but not actively angry) are about 60% of the workforce. This is what I will focus on in this book. These employees are the ones worth the effort and will give you an amazing return on your investment into them.

A word of caution; there is no magic pill. There is no One And Done solution. There are steps and initiatives that are needed from the top to the bottom and some from bottom to top. Changes, which all must happen with full corporate buy-in, need to be implemented on a personal and individual level, by *each* manager and team leader.

Unless your company is totally dependent on robots, and those robots are also fixed by other robots — you need to take care of the people that work for you! You need to take care of them more then you take care of your machines and even your money. If you do not take care of your employees, you will lose them and you will lose that money you are working so hard to get.

So, *what are you waiting for?*

Let's start working on the problem . . . but first . . . read this book so you are well prepared.

Lead By Engagement

No More Excuses:
Improve Your Engagement!

Employee Engagement

An extensive Gallup poll survey showed that 7 out of 10 of employees and managers in the USA are either disengaged with their work or actively disengaged, meaning either they are doing just enough to get by or they intentionally act in ways to negatively impact their organizations. This is costing US companies hundreds of billions of dollars each year. The annual cost nationwide to employ this actively disengaged group, which is 16% of the total workforce, exceeds $300 billion annually!

What's the cost of disengagement in *your* organization?

How can you engage your employees and managers?

What exactly is the meaning of being engaged?

Lead By Engagement

According to the Collins English Dictionary:

<u>En-gage: Verb Transitive</u>
(ɛnˈgeɪdʒ ; engājˈ; ɪnˈgeɪdʒ ; ingājˈ)

To attract and hold interest; to draw
into; involve
To pledge; to interlock with

What is employee engagement anyway?

Let's see what Gallup actually measures:

Every two to four years Gallup completes meta-analysis research — a statistical technique that pools multiple studies. In 2016, Gallup conducted its 9th meta-analysis using 339 research studies across 230 organizations in 49 industries and 73 countries. Within each study, Gallup researchers statistically calculated the work-unit-level relationship between employee engagement and performance outcomes that the organizations supplied.

Lead By Engagement

Combined, these researchers studied 82,248 work units, including nearly 1.9 million employees. This latest iteration of the meta-analysis further confirmed the well-established connection between employee engagement and key performance outcomes:

- customer ratings
- profitability
- productivity
- turnover (high & low turnover)
- safety incidents
- shrinkage (theft)
- absenteeism
- patient safety incidents
- quality (defects)

The 2016 meta-analysis verified once again that employee engagement relates to each of the nine performance outcomes studied. Gallup also found that the strong correlations between engagement and performance are highly consistent across different organizations from diverse industries and regions of the world.

Employee engagement does not mean just employee happiness. Someone might be happy at work because of the social connections and easy workload, but that doesn't necessarily mean they are engaged with work and are working hard or are being productive.

I have seen companies that have elaborate company programs for employees having a good time. While company game rooms and free massages are fun — and may be beneficial for other reasons — making employees happy is different from getting them engaged.

Lead By Engagement

One definition of engagement that I really like is:

> **Employee engagement is the emotional commitment the employee has to the organization and its goals.**
> **-- Kevin Cruise**

The key words here are *Emotional* and *Commitment*. This emotional commitment means engaged employees actually care about their work and their company. They don't work just for a paycheck or for the next promotion; they work on behalf of the organization's goals. This happens when employees know why they are working for the company. The purpose of their work is clear and in line with their personal goals and ideals.

When employees care — when they are engaged — they use discretionary effort. This means an engaged HR executive works overtime when needed, without being asked. This means an engaged mechanic cleans the shop floor where they work, even if the boss isn't watching.

I have been working in the areas of employee motivation, performance and productivity for many decades. The terms used to define performance and productivity have changed over time, but the reality remains the same. Although engagement is the buzz word now, it means the same thing: an inspired and motivated employee that is dependable and performing at above average level consistently.

Lead By Engagement

During my work I also observed that there were always some employees that had this *winner* attitude in them. They were helpful, willing to volunteer and always excelled in whatever they did. On the other hand, there were the ones that were the exact opposite. Both of these types were very few in number. Most of the employees were the ones that came to work on time, mostly, and left on time, mostly. They did the tasks they were given and lived a "normal" work life.

My observations led me to the conclusion that about 70-80% of employees are normal workers. They try to justify, in their own mind, the salary they receive. They work better and harder in certain situations and less and with lower quality in other situations. They need constant motivation and reasoning for their sporadic engagement. In my view, only about 10-15% of employees are the really engaged employees. They are the champions, the ones that excel no matter what they do – no matter what the work day brings. They have a desire to perform. They will be fully engaged, no matter what.

Then there are the bottom 10-15%, these are the actively disengaged. The troublemakers. They will find a reason to grumble and be toxic no matter what. They will use every opportunity to spread that toxicity to others. They will rarely respond to any motivational initiative, and any positive change is quickly lost. This actively disengaged group is generally noticeable. Dealing with this group needs a completely different approach, which is beyond the scope of this book.

From my perspective, the major issue is with staff that appear normal and come to work daily and have more or less a normal routine yet they are disengaged: they are the zombies at work. They work just enough to

Lead By Engagement

get by and sometimes fly under the radar of a manager because they are *not* troublemakers. These people are always looking at their watch for time to go home or start the weekend. These are the disengaged employees that *can* be reached and motivated! And the sad reality is . . . this is the majority, about 60%, of the total workforce. This group is not easily detectable. Managers and leaders need to be full engaged and work as manager/coaches to figure them out and provide an environment and inspiration to get them to evolve into fully engaged employees.

In most cases, when we use the term inspired or motivated employee, we think of it as time bound. Like someone is inspired to take a certain single action. The word engaged is used to define a person and not just the behavior, like engaged employee, which defines an employee as a good and high performing person . . . although this may not actually be the case. The commitment and motivation does not last forever, the same with engagement. As my mental mentor, Zig Ziglar, use to say:

> "People often say that motivation doesn't last. Well, neither does bathing – that's why we recommend it daily."

The point is that employee engagement or long-term employee motivation and commitment to their work is not a simple *one and done* issue. This is big and complex. It is as complex as people themselves. We know that people are different. They do not act or feel the way we think they should. What is obvious and natural to one, is unreasonable and difficult to another.

Lead By Engagement

On one hand, employee engagement is a corporate issue that needs corporate level thinking, support and strategic planning. It cannot be cured by any one magic pill (one half a day workshop). It needs a "cocktail" with constant monitoring and changes of the mixture.

On the other hand, employee engagement is also an individual issue. It is different from employee to employee. There cannot be one blanket approach to resolve this issue and both employer AND employee must work to update their mental connection to their work.

Employees are the most important resource that you have. That is why they must be taken care of. Also, they must not be "wasted." Human resources can be wasted in different ways. One way could be that you have employees that are not engaged as they do not feel appreciated — then they quit the job. Another way is that employees are working but not using their full potential, they are under-utilized, they are dis-engaged.

In this book I want to discuss this topic with my personal take on the subject, based on my experience and that of others with whom I have worked closely over the years. This book will present many ideas and possible solutions but they all depend on your own unique situation and will demand that you personalize each solution to your situation. What works for one may not work for another and to add some complexity to the mix: what works now may not work a year from now. You must stay engaged and fluid and flexible in order to make your business strong and grow it into the future.

I have also divided the possible solutions into strategic and tactical categories. The things that needed to be done corporately to change the environment and the approach. Also, I address the small things with big

Lead By Engagement

effects, these small things can be implemented by any team leader for themselves and their team. When only 26% of your employees are engaged with their work, what kind of results can you realistically expect?

> When only 26% of your employees are engaged with their work, what kind of results can you realistically expect?

Engaging leaders and good managers know how to boost their team's discretionary effort — extra time and energy employees **willingly** give to achieve their team's goals . . . and they have fun doing it!

The first step in the journey is yours. Engaging leaders start with themselves. They make sure that they are engaged with their employees before they start to expect their employees to be engaged with their work. In other words, they lead by example and by walking their talk. It is easier said than done, especially if you leaders have the habit of working in a certain way which is not conducive to creating engagement. And face it — most leaders are very success and metric driven, and expect people to take care of their own emotional involvement — learning to engage employees used to feel like a waste of work time — until you go back and look at those alarming statistics . . . Until you realize that you will make MORE money if your employees love their jobs.

Lead By Engagement

Even more difficult is when a leader is getting mediocre results and they are okay with that. Although the results are far lower than the potential, this type of leader is used to lower productivity and so they view it as a normal parameter. This happens in any organization with historically low morale and high turnover. In these cases the leader may not even realize that there is a problem let alone a solution.

As a performance and leadership trainer and coach, I have seen many organizations, both small and large, where the leaders and the employees are disengaged but don't even realize it. Disengagement became the culture and thus became the normal for all involved. I talked to the owners of such small companies about the low productivity and the negativity of the attitudes shown by staff. Their answers were similar and showed their own dis-engaged attitude. They blamed all the issues on the low quality of employees and were okay about low productivity and high turnover. This was normal for them and they didn't know what to do about it in any case.

In today's highly competitive business world, all organizations are looking for some competitive advantage to get ahead and stay ahead of the competition. The most important ingredient in this fight is people. The people are your employees, they are managers, they are customers and they are YOU. If you are engaged and can engage your people, you will have a competitive advantage that will be very hard to copy.

Tom Peter, management consultant and author, says that, "If your company is going to put customers first, then you must put employees *more* first."

If you care about your customers, which you should, you then have to take care of your team

Lead By Engagement

members and employees even more diligently. Realize, these employees are actually the ones that are going to take care of your customers and will be your face and voice in front of the world.

> "Thought,
> not money,
> is the real business capital."
> — Henry S. Firestone

REMEMBER, customers buy from people and not from companies. The statistics show that the majority of buying decisions are based on positive human interaction with sales staff. Also, another important US statistic is that in 2015 78.9% of all US gross domestic product came from the service industry — all are *delivered by people to people.* So the people in your organization and the performance that they deliver are the real competitive advantage for your company.

Thought comes from people, and not just any people, but the ones that are engaged. ENGAGEMENT is the key to success for you and your company.

All good leaders inspire. When you inspire your employees and they are engaged with their work, then the employees work better, harder and when necessary even longer hours. But the 300 billion dollar question is: how to engage the employees?

There are many things that can be done. Some are universal in nature and are set up so that anyone can put them in motion and reap the benefit and others are suggestions that may suit one company yet not another.

Lead By Engagement

Strategic steps that anyone can and must take are as follows:

1) Get yourself engaged with your employees and team. Then and only then can you expect that they will get engaged with their work. How will you do this? If you knew how, you would have done that already. Right? In the upcoming chapters I will show you how.

This is a self-development issue. The next chapter in the book is about self-development and becoming a true leader. If you are the owner of a company or a manager of department and you want to shine, you have to be a leader. Leadership is a combination of various skills. Personality and emotional intelligence are the key areas that any good leader must be trained and educated in. I have dedicated one chapter each for these two topics.

2) Get your team engaged. Again, how can you do this? You have done your self-development. You now have to communicate with your employees and team members. Try to understand them better. Again, understanding their personality and their emotional needs will come in handy. But first of all, you have to understand what an ***employee*** is. Well, an employee is a person. So, what is meant by a person? When you hire a person, what exactly is it you hire? I'll discuss this in detail.

Lead By Engagement

3) Tom Ziglar, President of Ziglar Inc. and son of American Legend Zig Ziglar, says that, "If your employees start working for a dream and not just a paycheck – everything changes." What is a dream? Dreaming is the emotional connection of a person with their future and/or passion. This is my definition of a dream. When you dream about being somewhere in life or having something, you get emotionally attached to it. It is not a reality yet, but it appears like a reality. I will discuss the importance of dreams and also teach you how to capture that passion.

Later in this book, I will have a number of tactical steps that you can take to improve team engagement and to ensure higher productivity resulting in higher ROI (Return on Investment) for your company.

A Better You!

As a leader and as a person, you need to continuously improve yourself. If you are reading this book, you have realized that there is something that needs to change.

Any kind of improvement in any area is nothing but a change to something different and better. If all is well, there is no need to improve or change. Am I right? Or Am I right?

Before you start on the journey of self-improvement, remember that any kind of improvement is a process and not an event. It is not one and done. However, there has to be a starting point and an ending point, otherwise how would you know what have you achieved?

The first step in self-improvement that I have always recommended and found to be highly result oriented, is to have couple of assessments done. These assessments show your starting point and uncover the areas that you are strong in and those in which you need to develop.

Remember you are the leader, what you do and how you do it affects many. You are improving not only for your sake but for the sake of your company and all the people that are affected by what you do and how you do it.

Lead By Engagement

As a leadership trainer/coach and with my experience of leading teams, I strongly recommend that you have an emotional intelligence assessment done. The most effective EI assessment that I can recommend is EQ-i 2.0 or EQ 360. These assessments will analyze your strengths in all the 15 EI areas that are most important in successful leadership and team work. Your assessment can pinpoint the areas you need to work on and the strengths that you have and how you can leverage these to overcome the less strong areas of your people skills.

The second assessment that I recommend is a personality assessment. This assessment can also do miracles in your personal and business relationships. I will discuss these assessments in detail. You will see that knowing yourself and your employees can really help you communicate and work with them much better.

Personality assessments come in many types. I have been licensed in two of these:

1) DiSC
2) Pearman Personality Integrator, which is more comprehensive and APA (American Psychological Association) approved.

These assessments will help you know yourself and identify your feelings and how others see you. Have you ever experienced that while you are talking and discussing something very normally, the other person asks you the reason for you being so upset, and you reply by saying you are not upset? The other person was

Lead By Engagement

perceiving something totally opposite than what you were trying to communicate. This is our personality and EI at play. You must be aware of your emotions and how they are impacting others if you want to actually communicate successfully.

Zig Ziglar has said:

WHAT you are and WHERE you are is because of what has gone into your mind. You can CHANGE what you are and where you are by Changing what goes into your mind.

That is why I strongly recommend that you take good care of your mental diet. Control the inputs so you can control your outputs.

Frank Outlaw said…
When you Change your THINKING,
You change your BELIEFS.

When you change your beliefs,
You change your EXPECTATIONS.

When you change your expectations,
You change your ATTITUDE.

When you change your attitude,
You change your BEHAVIOR.

When you change your behavior,
You change your PERFORMANCE.

Lead By Engagement

When you change your performance,
You change your LIFE.

I will add one sentence to it like this:

When you change YOUR LIFE.
You help change MANY LIVES.

Being a leader, you can make a difference to and for your staff and customers — and that difference is more profound than you may think. Be genuinely interested in improving other people. Those people will help you achieve your goals.

The following profound words are attributed to many different people with slight variations. This particular quote variation is attributed to Frank Outlaw, as well:

Watch your THOUGHTS, they become WORDS
Watch your words they become ACTIONS
Watch your actions, they become HABITS
Watch your Habits, they become your CHARACTER
Watch your Character, it becomes your DESTINY

Zig Ziglar is my mental mentor, as you realize by reading this far. I also am a Ziglar certified trainer. Zig has changed over a quarter of a billion lives around the world. He was really big on personal development. He was genuinely interested in people. He taught me that I have to be what I preach. Zig said, "You have to be before you can do, and you have to do before you can have." In order for you to expect your employees to be engaged in their work, you have to be engaged with them. This is your work because you are the manager

Lead By Engagement

and the leader — in this day and age, that is the very definition of manager and leader; if you are not developing and learning how to inspire — then you are not doing your job.

If you want to have a different life, different business or different habits you obviously have to do some things differently. As a company owner, manager and a leader, you have to lead differently. Get involved and get to know your employees. The results *will* be different (and better).

Self-improvement and/or self-development needs self-discipline. I never had that. I used to be one of the most disorganized persons who was only consistent in my inconsistency. If I could have become disciplined and consistent, I would have, but I never knew how. I knew that I needed that, I had the realization and the will to improve, but I just didn't know how. I read books, went to seminars, but I couldn't figure out how to change what was going on in my work world. Then I met a person who understood my problem and she became my accountability partner and a coach. That changed everything. It was not easy. Your old-self knows you really well. Knows your weak spots, your blind spots and won't like to vacate the comfortable dwelling for the new-you.

You know it is not easy to learn new habits, what is even harder is to get rid of the old one. You can do it. Just put your heart and mind to it.

Lead By Engagement

Let's see the steps required in your self-improvement:

1) Do the EI and Personality Assessments
2) Make a self-development plan — one area at a time
3) Have an accountability partner
4) Find a coach
5) Avoid negative input
6) Claim small victories
7) Be your own cheerleader

A Full Person

> The greatest power that a person possesses
> is the power to choose,
> — J. Martin Kohe

During my management days and later as a trainer and coach, I realized and observed that most managers can handle hard work, long hours, complicated technology, excessive travel and tough deadlines but they get bogged down when facing "difficult people." Managing and inspiring people in the long term is generally the biggest challenge for any manager and organization. In my view, the problem occurs because many organizations do not consider the employee as a ***full person.***

In most cases, each employee is only seen in relation to the job they are hired for. Let me explain this further. Suppose you have been hired as a telephone operator and your job is to answer the phones physically. You pick up the phone, you speak on the phone, you connect the call to the right person and you even write messages and then convey these to the right person. Now, since most of the work you are doing is physical, the manager sees you as a "physical person." But are you just a physical person? Are you a less of a person in comparison to say, a computer programmer or a music composer? No, you are not! None of the people

Lead By Engagement

working in the organization are any less or more of a person than each other.

American management and leaders mostly ignore this fact. They regard a worker in a factory (like a machine operator) as just a physical person. A supervisor or a computer programmer as a "mental person." Or in some cases they regard a team leader or concept writer as combination of a "physical and mental person." Based on this thinking any incentive and motivational plans are also designed to nourish and inspire just the physical and mental needs of these persons.

Remember, everyone has the power to choose. If they cannot choose the environment they are working in or the boss they are working for, they can definitely choose to like or dislike that. Based on their choice they will get engaged or disengaged with the work. If they feel de-motivated — the quality and quantity of their work will suffer.

Many companies that I worked for have elaborate programs to make sure that the sitting posture of a telephone operator or IT employee is correct so that their backs do not have issues. Similarly, there are brain storming sessions to feed the mind and create an atmosphere conducive for creative thinking. I have observed that most companies take care of the needs of their employees to the extent of the job they are performing. However, most of the time, because these people are not regarded as a full person, all of their needs are not understood nor catered to. To the employee it feels they are only receiving attention or assistance to get the job done, that there is no real concern for them as a human — no one reaching them from someone who wants to be considered a leader.

Lead By Engagement

The way I see it is that all people are full persons and a full person is a combination of four aspects:

1) Physical
2) Mental
3) Emotional
4) Spiritual

Unless all of the aspects of a full person are motivated, you will not get the kind of passionate performance each company is actually looking for. What is happening is that these leaders are in fact hiring a full person, but thinking of that person only as a partial person, and thus only receiving partial performance from that person. That is why there is disengagement among the workforce.

When a company hires a person, it pays that person a certain salary and expects the tasks of a certain job description to be performed. Most job descriptions now include something about being passionate about the role and job. However, in actual life, the job description is more about *quantity* of work rather than the *quality*. Even if the quality of performance is mentioned in the job description, the incentive or inspiration is not always there.

As a response to this, many employees are disengaged and working only the portion of that job description that they have to achieve in order to survive and keep their job. This wouldn't happen if the leadership was engaged and understood that all employees are full persons and need inspiration to become fully engaged in the work. Staff must be regarded as fully human and any motivation plan as well as most work conditions must be conducive to the

Lead By Engagement

utilization of all the aspects of each worker and manager.

Assembly line workers can be emotionally motivated to be engaged and thus use their hearts to perform better, and their hearts will feed their minds to help think about and improve the processes or recommend steps that may reduce waste but most certainly will reduce absenteeism.

If leadership is paying a full salary and receiving partial performance because the heart and mind of a worker is "unemployed," the company is losing. Remember the estimated $300 billion loss to US corporations in one year due to actively disengaged employees? That doesn't even include the loss due to the 58% of employees that are just disengaged. Isn't this something really serious that we all need to think about correcting?

In my consulting work, I have dealt with a large number of employees that were disengaged and most of the time those disengaged and actively disengaged employees were the ones who were, in my opinion and observation, more intelligent and also more enthusiastic (at one time) than most. However, because the leadership of the company never appreciated that intelligence and enthusiasm (emotional power) and did nothing to feed these aspects, they became disengaged as they discovered through experience that their ideas, passion and enthusiasm had no meaning for their leadership. If you are the leader of that group, wouldn't you do something to improve that situation?

The 4 aspects of a full person have certain details in common across all employees. A full person means that each person is a combination of the following four aspects:

Lead By Engagement

1) Physical – Using body, hands, legs, eyes, ears to do the job and needs motivation to use these.

2) Mental – Having brain and ideas, uses intellect to solve problems, plan and perhaps invent as well. Person also needs motivation to generate ideas and use the thinking power of the brain.

Almost all managers understand up to this level, however, not all know that there are two more aspects of all humans that the managers must understand and cater to if they want full utilization of their human talent in both quantity and quality and to get the passionate performance they really expect.

3) Emotional – Organizations and managers must look after many emotional aspects to really unleash the potential of their employees. This cannot happen unless the managers themselves are aware of and are trained in Emotional Intelligence. This is the missing link, this is the Game Changer. EI can bring the qualitative transformation in the organization to take it to the next level in today's highly competitive business world. Emotions can never be separated from any human. The brain is a combination of a thinking and a feeling brain. Emotions and feelings can never be over emphasized. The feeling and

Lead By Engagement

emotional part is the *why* for everything we do.

4) Spiritual – Some research has also discovered that the mind is actually a link between the physical and the spiritual human being. Although spiritually is more of a personal issue rather than an organizational one, it is highly recommended that organizations respect the spiritual needs and beliefs of their employees. Spirituality is closely linked to the emotional brain.

Now, let us examine a hypothetical situation:

You and a friend are hired by a person to dig some holes and you will be paid per hour at the current minimum wage. You are hired for two days. So, your wage for two days at minimum wage is locked in at a fixed amount. As you reach the yard where you are to dig holes, you are provided with the tools and are asked to dig a hole four feet in diameter and six feet deep. The soil is soft and you dug the hole in about two hours. You tell the boss that the hole is done. The person comes, inspects the hole and tells you to fill it. You are little confused, but you fill the hole. Then he tells you to dig a hole of the same specification about three feet away. You do it and when finished, the person comes inspects the hole and ask to you fill it. You get more confused, little unsure, still you do it. The guy then asks you to dig another hole of the same specification close by. This is repeated. After four holes you start doubting his mental

Lead By Engagement

health and lose all motivation and your 4th or 5th holes take you over half a day to dig . . .

Picture yourself digging those holes and think how you would really feel. You wanted the work, you got the work. You are getting the salary that you agreed upon. You are doing the work you agreed upon. But are you motivated? Are you engaged? How do you feel and why?

Now your boss sees that confused and perplexed look on your face. He takes you into his confidence and says, "Listen up, many years ago my dad buried a box full of old family memorabilia somewhere here. It is of great emotional value to me. I just found out about it by reading his diary. He passed away a year ago. I need your help to find that, so will you please keep on digging until we find it?"

Now, did anything change? How do you feel now? How is your engagement level after knowing more about the emotional purpose of your job?

Although you are a minimum wage worker, you are a full person. You have your emotional power, your mental power and your physical power. Since your boss gave respect, thought of you as a full person, involved you and gave you the reason why; you now have a purpose and you are suddenly engaged. Now you might also apply your other knowledge and abilities and suggest a metal detector to find the right place to dig for the box. Your boss now doesn't have to tell you where to dig, because you will start doing it in a logical way because now you know why you are working.

Lead By Engagement

If you want your employees engaged, think of them as a full person and help them work for a purpose and a dream. They will work passionately when their hearts and minds are engaged.

The steps in engaging your employees and team members are:

1) Get engaged yourself with your employees
2) Think of your employees as ***full persons***
3) Understand your employees and their needs
4) If they only work for a paycheck – help them have a dream

...again never underestimate the power of a dream!

Lead By Engagement

Dare to Dream!

It All Starts with a Dream

> "It may be that those who do most, dream most."
> — *Stephen Butler Leacock*

A dream changes everything. It is the job of the leader and the management of any group to give or develop a dream for all employees. If the dream is in line with the company's goals, miracles will happen. Imagine this: Your company is making 1 million in revenue when you have only 26% of your employees engaged. Now that you have put in an highly effective engagement program that engaged both your managers and employees, now you have 52% of your employees engaged. Where do you think your revenue will go? It will double or may triple. You have the same equipment, you are making/selling the same products, you have the same employees, same payroll, but you have lower turnover, higher morale and have increased your revenue!

Now comes another billion-dollar question. What is a dream and how can you sell one to your employees?

Lead By Engagement

Well, these are technically two questions. Let us consider the first part of the question here and now, and that is: what I mean by a dream.

Dreams are powerful. Dreams are like personal assets. Others may not see the value in these but for the dreamer it is their connection with the future and their personal passion. Some of the dreams are of a personal nature for their own life and that of their loved ones. I call them personal dreams and some dreams are big that can change the world.

"I have a dream," said Dr. Martin Luther King Jr. It was a dream that changed the USA for good. It was a dream indeed, no one could have really thought that the USA would change so much as to have a black president in the next few decades. Most people regarded it as madness, other as a ridiculous concept that whites and blacks should have same the rights. But it did happen, little by little, against all odds and severe resistance. There was another dream seen by Nelson Mandela, it seemed like a mad man's dream that one day blacks would rule their own country of South Africa which was under Apartheid at the time. These were BIG dreams of global magnitude, and absolutely unfathomable for most people, but they came true.

George Bernard Shaw wrote that "the reasonable man adapts himself to the world: the unreasonable one persists in trying to adapt the world to himself. Therefore, all progress depends on the unreasonable man."

Wow! Profound.

A little over one hundred years ago, it was a generally held view that you could not catch voices from the wind and hear people speak who were hundreds of miles away. It took the invention of the radio to

Lead By Engagement

challenge this view and to change the world. Today, you can not only hear a person across the globe, you can see them as easily as though they were seated next to you. The internet and television have made this possible.

Who would have believed in the 1800s that humans would be able to fly faster than any bird in the 1900s and beyond? The Wright brothers did. They challenged the view of their day and dared to dream. They were unreasonable men.

All the people that have changed the world in a big way were unreasonable people. Being unreasonable is being senseless, not level-headed, illogical or impractical.

Sensibility, practicality, level-headedness and logic are good qualities and qualities that are invaluable to any dreamer as they pursue their dreams. But while it is good to be like that when you are actually working on your dream, it is not advisable when it comes to defining your ultimate dream.

The point here is that when you are dreaming do not let any kind of restrictions stop you from the imagination of what will make your world a better place. Do not fall into the trap of possibilities, because the impossibilities become possibilities with time. Your ultimate dream should be unreasonable and outlandish. If it is not, you are not dreaming big enough. When you have a dream that is big enough it will be totally mind-blowing. It will be one that will challenge you and scare you at the same time. It will be a dream that is so huge you will get excited and question your own sanity at the same time.

I have been a dreamer and a thinker since I was very young. My dreams were more in the category of personal dreams and not the big impersonal kind that

Lead By Engagement

have potential to change the world. My dreams were big but only of the magnitude to change my life and do things that were impossibilities under the circumstances of my own environment and my physical condition. I was born severely asthmatic, I hated milk since birth and thus had severe calcium deficiency which manifested in various illnesses. I used to dream and I used to reject them because I found them to be impossible.

That is exactly the problem for us as leaders in today's business climate. Dr. Moses wrote about us being too sensible with our dreams. We plan according to what we perceive by our senses to be the truth. We plan according to how much money we see in our bank accounts or pockets, what we hear people say about us and our situation or the economy, and the resources and things we can touch as being available to us. We are restricted by our senses.

Yet, our senses were never designed to perceive spiritual, mental or abstract things. Our dreams begin with our thoughts — which are part of a mental process. Our thoughts are, or should be, superior to our senses. Whatever is manifested in the physical realm to the senses begins in the mental or spiritual realm.

If you are a dreamer you have to place more trust in your thoughts than in your senses. You must be unreasonable and senseless. Then your mind will be free to dream and to explore the possibilities of your potential.

Free yourself from your current physical limitations such as how much money you have, what papers you have, your current job, where you live and what you own. Your dream should be illogical and definitely not practical. If you have a clear idea right from the start as to how you could achieve your dream with every detail

Lead By Engagement

worked out, it is flawed, something in that dream is too small.

If you have a dream that is big enough, you will not know how you will achieve it all when you start. Sure, you will have an idea of where to begin, but not the whole picture of how to get to the finish line. The how is not important at this point, only the what. It's cliché, but take heed of the saying: where there is a will, there is a way.

Dr. Moses has suggested an "acid test" for your dreams. According to him: if most people agree with you that your dream is achievable and that it is reasonable, chances are it is not worth dreaming about. If, on the other hand, when you tell people your dream and they look at you like you have two blue heads, then you are probably on the right track.

Do not be limited by an inability to see beyond your present circumstances. Do not be controlled by your senses.

Dr. Moses also said that as a dreamer, you must realize that life is lived from the inside-out and not from the outside-in. It all starts in the mind. That is the real battlefield of life. That is where the war is raging. If you can create your ideal life in your mind and live that life like a reality every day in your mind, you have won the battle. It will have no choice but to manifest itself in the physical world.

Success, riches, happiness, fulfillment, recognition and all these goals, do not come as a surprise to dreamers when they get those things — because they have been living it in their minds all along. It had to happen. The physical world cannot resist the spiritual and mental worlds. In the hierarchy of life, it was

Lead By Engagement

designed so. One has to obey the other. The physical has to obey the spiritual and mental.

The spiritual and mental aspects of a person are limitless, boundless, free in every respect and more powerful than we could ever understand. They are unreasonable and senseless. Learn to utilize this power within you. You are all you can be. Go on and be it.

> BE UNREASONABLE

In his book, *Put Your Dreams To Test,* John Maxwell says that "a dream is an inspiring picture of the future that energizes your mind, will, and emotions, causing you to do everything you can to achieve it."

An inspiring picture becomes the catalyst for your mind, body and soul to find energy in order to get empowered to do everything to make that dream come true.

There are no restrictions or limitations on dreaming. You simply let your mind drift. This is called free association. Your mind drifts free from one idea to another and that idea leads to yet another and your mind associates one thought to the next.

Most people I know who achieved any level of significance in life had a dream. A dream that appeared unachievable, perhaps even unrealistic in the beginning. However, because they did not let go of that dream and worked towards achievement with consistency, they achieved it. You can also re-dream when you have achieved the original one or when your exposure increases or circumstances change.

Lead By Engagement

In many cases people put limitations on their dreams; so much so that they cannot even visualize the future as being better — they are stuck in a life rut. I remember reading that the childhood dream of former president Richard Nixon was to become a train engineer. That was the maximum that he could dream at that age. Another example is that Zig Ziglar, the American legend who transformed hundreds of millions of lives, had a childhood dream of owning a butcher shop in his home town. But later in 1952 he had a new dream. His new dream was to become a motivational speaker and it took him almost 20 years before he realized this dream. He went through thick and thin but never gave up on the new and improved dream.

Dreams get you going, they give you the inspiration to get up every morning and go to work even when it is raining or snowing, hot or cold, come hell or high water. You have to have a dream . . . and a big one too.

> "Dare to Dream big dreams; only big dreams have the power to move men's souls."
> — Marcus Aurelius

The first secret of becoming significant is simple: Dream Big Dreams!

Allow yourself to dream. Allow yourself to imagine and fantasize about all your career goals and the kind of life you would like to live. Think about the amount of money you would like to earn and what great things you can do for others and the community. All great people begin with a dream of something wonderful and different from what they had when they started to dream.

Lead By Engagement

You have to have a dream if you want to make a dream come true.

Imagine that you have no limitations on what you can be, have or do in life. Just for the moment, imagine:

. . . that you have all the power
. . . all the money
. . . all the time
. . . all the resources
. . . all the support and help

and everything else you need to achieve anything you want in life.

If your potential were completely unlimited, what kind of a life would you want to create for yourself and your family?

Here is what Brian Tracy says, "Practice 'back from the future' thinking. This is a powerful technique practiced continually by high-performing men and women. This way of thinking has an amazing effect on your mind and on your behavior." He explains how it works. "Project yourself forward five years. Imagine that five years have passed and that your life is now perfect in every respect. What does it look like? What are you doing? Where are you working? How much money are you earning? How much do you have in the bank? What kind of a lifestyle do you have?"

Create a vision for yourself for the future. The clearer your vision of your life, the faster you move toward it and the faster it moves toward you. However, in many cases you may not have a very clear picture, but don't worry. Dreams are not supposed to be that clear all the time. Have a dream and later it can become clearer

Lead By Engagement

as you know more and have more exposure to how life can change.

I am a dreamer and a thinker. I was always vague about my dreams, I had not converted them into what Howard Partridge referred to as "intentional dreams." I call them knitted dreams. Knitting your dreams is having a dream and it gets you so excited that you knit more of it and make your dreams clearer and even bigger and broader with this knitting. This is an intentional process but has much more emotions and feelings to it than just being built from intellect and planning. When you create a clear mental picture of where you are going in life and set clear goals, you become more positive, more motivated and more determined to make it a reality. You trigger your natural creativity and come up with idea after idea to help make your vision come true.

Imagine the time you were in the last semester of school or college and you had a dream of what you would be and what your life would be after school was finally finished. Or when you first fell in love or were about to get married or were thinking of getting married . . . you had a dream, an imagination . . . you could see yourself in the future and having an amazing life traveling together, raising a family and relaxing on the beach. You could really visualize it. In your imagination you see yourself doing and living a life of your dreams then you extend it and add new things and wishes to it. This is dream knitting.

Brian Tracy says that you always tend to move in the direction of your dominant goals, dreams, images and visions. The very act of allowing yourself to dream big dreams actually raises your self-esteem and causes you to like and respect yourself more. It improves your

Lead By Engagement

self-concept and increases your level of self-confidence. It increases your personal level of self-respect and happiness. There is something about dreams and visions that is exciting and that stimulates you to do better than you ever have before.

Brain Tracy has this wonderful technique . . . He wants you to think internally and ask and answer a great question over and over again: What one thing would you dare to dream if you knew you could not fail? If you were absolutely guaranteed of success in any one goal in life, large or small, short-term or long-term, what would it be? What one great goal would we dare to dream if we knew we could not fail?

Brian Tracy recommends that whatever it is, write it down and begin imagining that you have achieved this one great goal already. Then, look back to where you are today.

> ➢ What would you have done to get where you want to go?
> ➢ What steps would you have taken?
> ➢ What would you have changed in your life?
> ➢ What would you have started up or abandoned?
> ➢ Who would you be with?
> ➢ Who would you no longer be with?
> ➢ If your life were perfect in every respect, what would it look like?

Whatever it is that you would do differently, take the first steps today.

Dreaming big dreams is the starting point of achieving significance. The #1 reason that people never succeed is because it never occurs to them that they can

Lead By Engagement

do it. As a result, they never try. They never get started. They continue to go around in circles, spending everything they earn and a little bit more besides. They always wait for the perfect time and being great before they begin. But there is no perfect time and each moment is as perfect as the other. No one can ever be perfect. Perfection is never achieved, it is improvement that keeps on happening. I love a quote from Joe Sabah which Zig Ziglar also mentions in his books:

> "You don't have to be great to start but you have to start to be great."

When you begin to dream big dreams about success, you begin to change the way you see yourself and your life. Then you make your dreams intentional. You begin to do different things, bit by bit, gradually, until the whole direction of your life changes for the better. Dreaming big dreams is where greatness begins to happen.

Dreaming must come from your heart, it is something you feel. **You** then have to make your dreams into intentional dreams. Intentional dreams are the dreams that you have not only dreamt but also though about a lot. Not just while you are sleeping but also when you are awake. This is the first step towards making your goals happen. The first step in making your dreams into intentional dreams is to write them down. Zig Ziglar (who I never met but listened to him talk on CDs), called it the Dream List, others call it a Dream Board. A dream list is like a dream team. You do not consider that it is really possible to bring all those players together to play. But you still make a dream team to play baseball, football or soccer. You do not get

Lead By Engagement

into the discussion of possibilities and impossibilities, it is fun and a great exercise of the mind just to imagine your dream team.

For your dream list, don't think of possibilities and impossibilities either, just put your dreams there. You can write down everything, like maybe you want to become the President of the USA, start a global charity or have a multi-million dollar home on your favorite beach . . . or whatever your dream is. Just let it flow!

Howard Partridge in his book *Think and Be Phenomenal*, says that, "when your mind is free and open to associate, your subconscious mind begins working on the problem or idea for you." That is why, when you are really stressed out or bogged down about finding a solution for a problem, it is strongly recommended that you relax your mind, go and do something completely different and very soon new ideas and possible solutions will flow into your mind.

Coming back to the dream list topic. I would like you to stop reading this book any further for the next hour or so and do this exercise:

➢ Take a blank piece of paper and on the top write **My Dream List.**

➢ Below that write *Everything that I want to be, do or have.*

Lead By Engagement

Before I tell you the next step, read and think about this one quotation with a very important point and also one reminder for you:

*You are never too old
to dream a new dream,*

Reminder: sensibility, practicality, level-headedness and logic are good qualities, no doubt. They are qualities that are invaluable to any dreamer as they pursue their dreams. However, this is not the time for those types of skills, put those qualities away for later use. At this time, be a free spirit and really dream of your dream job, dream business, dream home, dream whatever you wish to be, do or have . . .

Now, go back to the blank paper with the headings you just put in and write the first dream, and then second . . . and then third . . . It may take you a few days to really do this exercise because you, like most people, will write your plans and goals *instead of* dreams and later will erase those and write your real dreams.

After you are done with this exercise and have tasted the benefits of this, have your team leaders do it for themselves and then help employees do it as well. This will change the way people see their work and their life. It will also allow all the different staff to realize everyone else in the company is a full person — a full person with wishes and dreams too. The dreams will make a connection with each person's personal life and work life and also connect the present with the future.

Lead By Engagement

Dream List

Everything . . . I think I want to be,
do or have...

Lead By Engagement

Dream Knitting

This term I have translated from my mother tongue Urdu, from my country of birth: Pakistan. This term is very frequently used in poetry and literature in my culture.

As I mentioned earlier, I have always been a dreamer and a thinker. As far back I can remember, I used to dream. These dreams got me excited; I use to knit those dreams into bigger and broader dreams and from those grander dreams I would, at times, knit totally new dreams.

Dream knitting is an intentional exercise, it is kind of day dreaming but if you really put your heart into it, it becomes an exercise that gives you the self-worth, confidence and enthusiasm to go after those dreams.

To me it has always been a self-motivational activity. I knit dreams and then the extensions. I could really see myself doing whatever I was dreaming and not only that, I could see myself achieve and feel the elation of the achievement. This mental picture would give me the motivation and enthusiasm that would push me to work towards those knitted dreams. Later I learned that knitted dreams must be written down as they grew bigger. In the beginning I would just write the part of the dream that was the achievement. But later I

Lead By Engagement

realized that the whole knitted dream is actually a really good motivational story.

So I started writing these stories. At times, I used to feel as if these were real stories and I had written my life in them. I used these stories to motivate myself and the people around me.

Most of my dreams were personal in nature. Howard Partridge in his book *Discover Your Phenomenal Dreamlife* says that there are two kinds of dreams the *personal* and *impersonal*. Personal dreams are those that impact your own life and impersonal dreams are the ones that impact other lives. Nelson Mandela, Dr. Martin Luther King Jr. — they all had impersonal dreams of global/national magnitude.

I also had impersonal dreams. With the grace of God, I have accomplished most of my personal dreams. My impersonal dreams are the ones I am working on now. Do you want to know about my impersonal dreams? . . . Here you go:

- ➢ I have a dream to be an author whose writing makes the readers realize their deep potential and the seeds of greatness in them.
- ➢ To be able to transform lives and spread happiness around the world.
- ➢ To help people find beauty in all aspects of our environment and love all of humanity.
- ➢ To make people realize the power of love and forgiveness.

I am knitting some new dreams as well and will tell you when the knitting is complete.

Lead By Engagement

I encourage you to knit your own dreams. Don't be shy, dreams will work as beacons for you, they will energize you.

What ingredients are required for knitting dreams? In my view the kind of dreams I am talking about need the following five ingredients, if you have these you can knit big dreams.

1) A dream
2) Free and open mind
3) Wild or unrestricted imagination
4) Positive attitude
5) Love

The Love as the 5th ingredient will make your dream knitting more emotional and an inside out activity. It will add more feelings and meanings to any dream.

This exercise for you is to build on the dream list that you created in the previous chapter. Zig Ziglar suggests to write on the same sheet — in one sentence — *why* you want that dream. If you cannot write it in one sentence then it is not a dream but a whim, get rid of it.

What I would like you to do is — after you have your why in there, write that dream and its why on top of a new sheet for each dream and then start knitting the dreams and make the connections intentional with your imagination.

See yourself in five years from now with that dream being achieved. Feel the feelings of that achievement. Think of the people who helped you in the process. The lessons you learned. What did you do? How did it

Lead By Engagement

impact your family and your loved ones? What was the impact on other people and society?

Do you feel elated? Do you feel thankful? Do you feel proud or humble? Do you feel accomplished?

So, write down the feelings and the whole story of your future success. This will take some time for each dream but it will give you the inspiration and energy to achieve those knitted dreams.

Now, for many of you, five years may seem like a very long period. Well, it depends on the dream. Actually, it may take a lesser or a longer time. The point is that you knit a dream and then you work towards it to achieve your dream life. Time will pass whether you act or you sit still. For the people in my age group, five years is a not a long time, especially when we look back in time.

Remember, time passes even if you do not have a dream or a goal. It is better to have a dream and a goal and take steps to make your life and the world a better place — no matter the size of the step you take. You will achieve something. Also, there is a general tendency in most of us to overestimate ourselves in the short term and underestimate ourselves in the long term. Do not be afraid of knitting long term dreams. Some dreams can only be realized over a longer period of time.

Do you remember when you were young you wanted everything *now*. As you grew older you learned that all things cannot happen *now*. Planning for something to happen in one year's time seemed like forever. Now, imagine if you had saved money little by little during your school and college . . . how much it would have been *now?* Similarly, if you gain knowledge just by reading just a few pages every day . . . how much would you have gained in the last 5 years of your life?

Lead By Engagement

Never underestimate the power of small but consistent effort.

An Urdu proverb says;
Sea is a combination of drops of water.

One really important point . . .

Dreaming is not the only step. It is the first step. Also, like most human developmental areas, this is not one and done. All improvement and engagement is a process and a way of work-life. Persistently consistent effort is required to engage people and *keep* them engaged.

After you knit your dreams, your company's dreams and help your employees with their dreams, you have to develop yourself to be a more effective leader and then help your teams and employees to become more effective and engaged.

The next chapters will help you do just that.

Lead By Engagement

Game Changer

"I did then what I knew how to do. Now that I know better, I do better."
— Maya Angelou

In earlier chapters I mentioned emotional intelligence and the EI assessments EQ-i 2.0 and EQ 360. In this chapter I will discuss in more detail emotional intelligence and what it can do for you and your employees.

All humans try to do better, try to make their life better as days go by. This is human nature. However, very few of us know *how* to become better. Mostly we learn from our mistakes. Trial and error is the most common way of learning how to live life. No college or university teaches us how to live a good life or how we can become a better person anyway.

In our work lives, most of the training people go through is about hard skills, technology and sales. As I mentioned earlier, during my management days and later as a trainer and coach, I realized and observed that most managers can handle hard work, long hours, complicated technology, excessive travel and tough deadlines, but they get bogged down when facing "difficult people." Managing and inspiring people in the

Lead By Engagement

long term is generally the biggest challenge for any manager and organization.

I was always interested in people. When I was an MBA student at the University of Missouri, I wanted to do my PhD in psychology or organizational behavior. It always intrigued me to learn how and why people behave the way they behave. Although life took me in a direction so that I never got to finish my PhD, I always worked with people and have a great record of motivating people. I inspired all the teams that I lead. Not only that, I developed great lasting relationships with them. I still have people that worked in my teams in the early 1980s as my Facebook friends and I still try to guide them whenever they need my guidance or advice.

I had one problem, I found it very difficult to work with difficult and unfair bosses. Since I was very fair with my teams and many a times I would take a strong stance for them and would take all the responsibility for their mistakes, I have little tolerance for any leader that doesn't at least try to be fair with their staff. I found it difficult to swallow that my boss would take credit and give blame for basically any project we worked on together. These incidences made me bitter and angry. This bitterness slowly grew in me and I became an angry worker. I got disengaged and at times actively disengaged. My results were still very good but I did not get the reward that I was expecting. I was rightfully disengaged as far as my thought process went, and it happened so slowly I didn't realize how my attitude and work behaviors were changing — slowing.

That was the time when I resigned and joined another company. The new company sent me to a training. During this training I met a lady; a professional trainer who was focused on soft skills and emotional intelligence. That was the first time I heard about EI or EQ (Emotional Intelligence or Emotional Quotient).

What is Emotional Intelligence?

There are several definitions of EI. According to Daniel Goldman "it is the capacity of recognizing our own feelings and those of others, for motivating ourselves, and managing emotions well in ourselves and in our relationships." (Daniel Goleman 1998.)

Reuven Bar-On, the creator of EQ-i 2.0, has defined EI as: "Emotional-social intelligence is a cross-section of interrelated emotional and social competencies, skills and facilitators that determine how effectively we understand and express ourselves, understand others and relate with them, and cope with daily demands." (Reuven Bar-On 2005.)

In simpler words, it is the capacity of understanding and controlling our emotions and those of others.

In a business environment, EI is proven to be a game changer. It is a combination of various skill sets that are absolutely essential for leadership in particular and success in life and work in general.

As a leader and a team player, you must be aware of how your emotions and feelings are being manifested. These manifestations make a certain impact on the people working with you. Many times you may not be aware of the tone, the face expressions, the body language or even the words that you are using. The people around you may take a totally different impression than what you wanted to express; and of which you may remain unaware. Emotionally Intelligent leaders and workers are conscious of their feelings, the impacts being created and the emotions of other.

Many leaders carry the frustration and anger of one meeting into another completely unrelated meeting unknowingly, and this creates problems for the team. If one is not emotionally intelligent, the mood swings and sudden reactions to an unaccepted event or information may result in demoralization of the team or even further negative reaction from someone on the team, creating a war of words that can get ugly.

Emotional intelligence has really proven to be a game changer for me. It changed who I was and how I was. I used to think and act differently.

I lived a life of self-doubt for a while and before that I was brimming with over-confidence. Emotions, both positive and negative, were controlling my mind and actions and via them my very life. When I was finally introduced to emotional intelligence, it was an epiphany moment for me. I realized that one can control one's emotions rather than be controlled by them. I learned it, practiced it in daily life and practically altered my life path, both on the personal and professional sides. Since I found it to be so transformative, I decided to develop myself in this area even further and help out as many people as I could.

I strongly believe (and this belief is based on the results that I and my clients achieved) that EI training is a must for all employees *of all levels.* It is even more a must for the leaders of teams of every size.

It is a fact that emotions and sentiments are inherent in whatever we think and do. It is impossible to be completely devoid of emotions. It is also equally important to have the intellect to perform various personal and professional functions in an efficient

Lead By Engagement

manner — aside from those existing emotions. As a matter of fact, any external stimulus from any of our senses passes through our emotional center before it reaches our thinking brain so we cannot and should not ignore emotions. In other words, whatever information is passed from our senses to our brain gets a "coating" of emotions on it. Nothing we think is free from an emotional bias at some level. That is the reason that the most rational thinking connected to the stock market fluctuates on the basis of sentiments and emotional reactions to the daily news. It is called market sentiment.

Have you ever been in a situation where you said or acted in a way that appeared very appropriate at the time, however, a few minutes or a day later you wondered how you could ever say or do such a thing? Anybody? . . . Nobody? Well, if you have not, you are a perfect human being, perhaps even an angel.

Unfortunately, many of us are not that perfect and a lot of times we do things that we regret doing later. I have been guilty of that once or twice in my life. Well, honestly, a lot more than once or twice.

Let's analyze such situations. When and why do they happen to you? What type of situations or circumstances make you do it? I can guarantee that each of those times was an emotionally charged event. You were most likely angry, elated, depressed or afraid.

Why is it that despite being smart and wise, we do or say things we would never say or do in our normal work or personal lives when suddenly hit by a strong emotion?

Psychologists call it ***emotional hijacking.*** They say that our emotions take control and make us act in these ways that later we regret. According to research, in emotional situations, our emotional brain (limbic

Lead By Engagement

system) produces a chemical that shuts down or severely weakens its communications with the thinking brain (neocortex). As a result, incoming information is not fully processed and the decision is performed by the emotional brain without the due process of our intellectual side.

Let's look at the following hypothetical business scenario to understand the decision process in our brain.

A sales rep who is lagging behind in target numbers for sales has to make a decision about reducing the price of a product to get a large order that will allow him to reach the sales goal or, because the year is coming to an end, stay below the goal and possibly not get a bonus that year. This sales rep does not have the authority to change the price. He must contact management in order to make that price change. The management has a larger picture they must consider for pricing decisions and will look at all the information from various angles before making a decision. The sales rep could not get in touch with management because their system was down. He drops the price because it appears to be the right choice under the circumstances. This resulted in the start of a price war with a close competitor and a loss to the company and bad name for that sales rep. Forget about the sales goal, now this rep might lose his job. If this sales rep could have communicated quickly with someone from management, the decision would have been different and better for all involved.

In the above scenario, the sales rep is the emotional brain (the limbic system), the management is the thinking brain (neocortex), the need to drop the price to achieve the target sales goal is the emotional situation. The downed system represents the communication

Lead By Engagement

shutdown between the two parts of our brains and the result was a lower quality decision.

The limbic system (emotional brain) is designed to create spontaneous decisions in a fight or flight situation. In sudden situations, the emotional brain takes over and we make abrupt decisions to save ourselves. We ***react*** instead of ***responding***. However, in normal situations the thinking brain remains in control to make better quality decisions in *collaboration* with the emotional brain (not despite of emotions).

The limbic system is used most frequently by animals since they rely on their instincts for survival. When we let our emotions take the driving seat, our behavior also becomes instinctive, reactive like animals.

However, later . . . when the dust settles and the information gets processed by the neocortex, we wish we had not done something or admit we should have done it differently. Some of us are more emotional (lower emotional intelligence) and are often faced with such situations. If not properly trained, these people don't even realize the problem, and think they are acting normally. This is even a bigger problem because they are both self-unaware and also unaware of the negative impact of their emotions and actions on others.

Emotions and intelligence are inherently present in us humans, and both complement each other. Emotional Quotient (EQ) is used to measure emotional intelligence just as intelligence quotient (IQ) is used to measure intelligence and problem-solving skills. Research says that our IQ cannot be changed after the age of 17; what changes after that age is our exposure and experience. However, our emotional intelligence can be improved and learned and strengthened regardless of age. Further, research has proven that EQ is a much better indicator of

Lead By Engagement

success in the workplace than IQ and is used to identify leaders, good team players and people who work best by themselves. Higher emotional intelligence will let you do everything better than lower emotional intelligence ever will.

Let us discuss the physiology of the brain. Look at the figure below, it will help understand better what I am trying to get at.

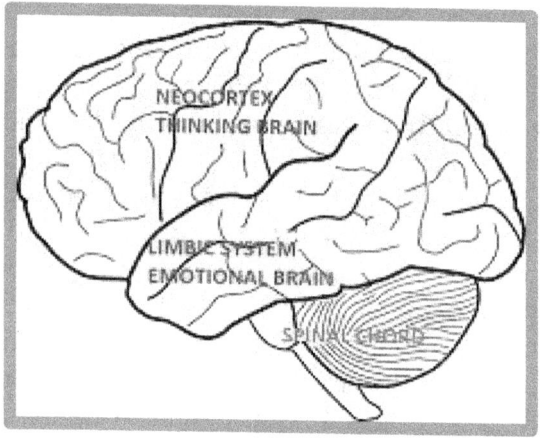

> Emotions reside in the limbic system which is much older in evolution than the neocortex where cognitive abilities (IQ) reside.
> Emotions came before thinking.
> We feel first and think later.

Lead By Engagement

The brain's emotion centers evolved first. The limbic system surrounds the brainstem. This is the center of passionate emotions and also influences learning and memory. Later evolution produced the neocortex where the brain thinks. Meanwhile, on the sides of the brain, there grew the amygdala, a pair of structures that act as a storehouse of our emotional memory. *The amygdala gives life emotional meaning and passion.* We treasure these parts of life as humans, but also as humans we can't let it rule our day-to-day decisions.

In a crisis, the amygdala reacts almost instantly, far more quickly than the neocortex. The basic instinct of fight or flight. Allowing our emotional brain to act independently of our thinking brain. The amygdala gives extra weight to memories of emotional arousal, so we have vivid memories of pleasure or danger. While the amygdala pushes us to action, the neocortex works like a damper. It stifles or controls feelings. It tries to put sense into the whole emotional and panicky scene. We experience emotional hijackings when the amygdala is triggered and the neocortex fails to control it. Strong emotions interfere with our attention span and every aspect of clear thinking.

Since we have briefly discussed how the emotional and thinking parts of our brain work, let us move forward to emotional intelligence and why it is a Game Changer.

Lead By Engagement

Psychologist Daniel Goleman, Ph.D. observed that:

- The notion that there is pure thought, rationality devoid of feeling, is a fiction. In terms of biological design for the basic neural circuitry of emotion, what we are born with is what worked best for the last 5,000 human generations, not the last 500 generations - and certainly not for the last five.
- We have feelings about everything we do, think about, imagine or remember.
- Thought and feeling are inextricably woven together. The question is, how can we bring intelligence to our emotions — and civility to our streets and caring to our communal life?
- IQ and emotional intelligence are not opposing competencies, but rather separate and complementary ones.

In the last 15 years of so, there has been a lot of research on emotional intelligence. Different EQ (emotional quotient — the measurement of EI) assessment tools and tests have been created. EQ is now believed to be a much better indicator of success in personal and professional life then IQ. Another great aspect of emotional intelligence is that it can be learned, changed and enhanced. Whereas an IQ level remains static after the age of 17 or 18. What increases after that is our exposure and experience.

The easiest way to understand emotional intelligence is to think of it as all the non-IQ areas of human intelligence. This covers personal and social intelligence involving the ability to monitor one's own emotions and the emotions of others and to use this

Lead By Engagement

information to guide one's thinking and action. Emotional intelligence (a combination of multiple skills) is emerging as the most important competency in business. In the business world, these interpersonal, managerial and leadership skills form the core of what separates star performers from the rest of the pack.

Years of solid academic research now support the intuitive truth that mastery of these personal and interpersonal competencies is the single most important factor when determining people's success in life in general. Emotional intelligence is vital for success in life and business. This is a combination of skills and senses that make us adept in dealing with stressful situations and difficult people.

Our brain is primitive. It is designed for fight and flight situations. In primitive times, when we were face to face with the enemy or our prey, the limbic system used to take over enabling us to take an instant decision of running or staying with adrenaline pumping to fight. In current stressful and competitive situations, our limbic system releases the same chemicals that take control of our thinking and therefore information does not fully circulate in our neocortex.

Now, the problem is that the brain is the same as it was thousands of years ago; with the same "wiring" and functionality. Under severe emotional situations like stress, anger, sadness, happiness or anxiety, the limbic system takes over and we act on instinct — but now in an office setting. However, there is no jungle, no war, no wild beast attacking you, but a conference room where a marketing plan is being discussed.

Our reactions to opposing views when we are under stress come out like these business discussions are a war. This is when emotional intelligence helps us to

Lead By Engagement

control our emotions and respond with deliberate action instead of reacting. It cools us down and allows the neocortex to work as a damper. That is how using our intelligence saves us from low quality decisions, emotional outbursts and protects us from being humiliated later. The key is to develop the habit of allowing our higher brain to take control.

Over the course of my professional life I have met many professionals who are masters in their area of expertise, however, developing a cohesive team that is engaged in their work remained a challenge for them. They got frustrated and blamed the situation on the bad attitude of the team members. Most of these managers were really good technical professionals but with no training in EI — they were abysmal failures in leading a team to success.

Similarly, I have met and later trained numerous workers that were disengaged and were bad team players. They could not get along with their fellow employees or their managers. The best example of before and after emotional intelligence training is no one else but *me*. I have been through all kinds of emotional ups and downs in my early professional life.

In the beginning, after my MBA degree, I was brimming with confidence, I was hard-working, passionate and highly result oriented. My bosses loved me because I used to get the job done. My co-workers and team members hated me because I didn't care about the people I was working with. To me the numbers and results were everything. In meetings I used to contribute the most, would not care about the impact I was making on the people around me. Slowly, my low EI started showing in my results. People started quitting. The results were not as good as they were in the beginning

Lead By Engagement

and the bosses were not happy. Now I became the culprit. I would put fault with the team and the workers and even the boss; but never my own style of leadership. Soon I suffered humiliation and I was let go. The same situation was repeated one more time.

Now I lost the confidence I started out with and became unsure of myself. I felt like I was a failure and not fit for the environment in the bigger corporations which I had planned to be my career. Sometimes I used to think I was right and everybody else was wrong and at other times, I was the problem. I became bitter and angry. My attitude and behavior became toxic. My family was also affected.

Emotional intelligence training developed in me self-regard, stress tolerance, empathy, optimism and impulse control. I became a better manager and a better person.

EI develops a balanced attitude. Highly task-oriented managers believe that emotions have nothing to do with business. They also claim that emotions make them weak managers. Because these managers are not fully aware of emotional intelligence and definitely not trained in it, they regard emotional intelligence as acting goody-goody with their employees. The over ambitious managers take a macho style of thinking as their strength.

Many leaders and managers do not know what impact their tone of voice, facial expressions and body language are creating on their team members. At times, when the managers are trying to show confidence and assertiveness, it can be misconstrued to be anger and arrogance. Similarly, untimely softness and certain body language can be taken as lack of commitment and uncertainty.

Lead By Engagement

EI is all about being conscious of your own emotions and what impact those feelings are creating on others. Similarly, it is about understanding the emotions of others and being in control of the situation.

In fact, EI develops assertiveness, decision making skills, independence and stress tolerance in you. However, it does it with a balanced approach by also keeping you aware of the impact these skills and capabilities are making on the team. The purpose of developing EI is simply to make you a more effective leader both in the short and long term.

In my experience, the leaders who resist EI, regarding it as not important or a waste of resources, have no understanding of what EI really is and what it can do for them. When not trained in emotional intelligence, these managers can become a source of creating disengagement. If you want your team members and workers to be engaged, you have to improve your own EI. Otherwise, you are responsible for the waste of your own capabilities and that of your team and company.

The major issue in many organizations is that the decision makers do not realize the underlying issue — which is a lack of emotional intelligence. As the famous inspirational speaker Zig Ziglar has said, "The first step in solving a problem is to recognize that it does exist."

In the last ten to fifteen years there has been a great deal of research on emotional intelligence. Psychologists have developed different assessments to measure emotional intelligence scientifically. These assessments measure various behavioral aspects and determine which aspects are fully developed and which should be improved. EQ-i 2.0 and EQ 360 are the most widely used assessments in business organizations to measure

Lead By Engagement

EQ. These are American Psychological Association (APA) level B assessments. In EQ-i 2.0, fifteen behavioral aspects are measured which are regarded as the indicators of our overall wellbeing and success, and are crucial for leaders.

This assessment measures 5 key areas with 3 essential skills in each of the area, with total of 15 critical skills/capabilities. All of these skills are needed to become a balanced and successful leader/team player. The EQ-I 2.0 model is given below, the competencies and skills are listed below for your information as well:

1) **Self-Perception**: Self Regard, Self-Actualization, Emotional Self-Awareness
2) **Self-Expression**: Emotional Expression, Assertiveness, Independence
3) **Interpersonal**: Relationships, Empathy, Social Responsibility
4) **Decision Making**: Problem Solving, Reality Testing, Impulse Control
5) **Stress Management**: Flexibility, Stress Tolerance, Optimism

Lead By Engagement

Copyright © 2011 Multi-Health Systems Inc. All rights reserved.
Based on the original BarOn EQ-i authored by Reuven Bar-On, copyright 1997

Lead By Engagement

EQ as a Competitive Business Asset

Emotional intelligence has become one of the most sought-after skill sets in corporate America today. When the Harvard Business Review published an article on the topic a few years ago, it attracted a higher percentage of readers than any other article published in that periodical in the last 40 years!

When the CEO of Johnson & Johnson read that article, he was so impressed that he had copies sent out to the 400 top executives in the company worldwide. It is as if so many people knew there was a problem yet couldn't define it — then they read the article and felt hope for their team again.

IQ and EQ

IQ by itself is not a very good predictor of job performance. Hunter and Hunter estimated that at best IQ accounts for about 25% of the variance. Sternberg has pointed out that studies vary and that 10% may be a more realistic estimate. On the other hand, research has shown that EQ accounts for up to 49% of a person's success at their work.

Lead By Engagement

An example of this research on the limits of IQ as a predictor is the Sommerville study, a 40 year longitudinal investigation of 450 boys who grew up in Sommerville, Massachusetts. Two-thirds of the boys were from welfare families, and one-third had IQ's below 90. However, IQ had little relation to how well they did at work or in the rest of their lives. What made the biggest difference was their abilities such as being able to handle frustration, control emotions and get along with other people.

Another good example is a study of 80 PhDs in scientific studies who underwent a battery of personality tests, IQ tests and interviews in the 1950s when they were graduate students at Berkeley. Forty years later, when they were in their early seventies, they were tracked down and estimates were made of their success based on resumes, evaluations by experts in their own fields and sources like American Men and Women of Science. It turned out that social and emotional abilities were four times more important than IQ in determining professional success and prestige.

The Business Case for EQ

Martin Seligman has developed a concept called learned optimism. It refers to the causal attributions people make when confronted with failure or setbacks. Optimists tend to make specific, temporary, external causal attributions, while pessimists make global, permanent, internal attributions. Optimism is a key ingredient of EI.

Lead By Engagement

Research at MetLife

➢ In research at MetLife, Seligman and his colleagues found that new salesmen who were optimists sold 37% more insurance in their first two years than did pessimists.

➢ When the company hired a special group of individuals who scored high on optimism but failed the normal screening, they outsold the pessimists by 21% in their first year and 57% in the second. They even outsold the average agent by 27%.

Research at the University of Pennsylvania

➢ In another study of learned optimism, Seligman tested 500 members of a freshman class at the University of Pennsylvania. He found that their scores on a test of optimism were a better predictor of actual grades during the freshman year than SAT scores or high school grades.

Lead By Engagement

Emotional Intelligence, improves your stress tolerance. It enables and empowers you to take and make higher quality decisions and not get bogged down or breakdown due to stress. Most emotional and lower quality decisions come in stressful situations. Also, EI improves your impulse control. I have observed that under stressful situations and as a result of a sudden unexpected event, leaders and managers react impulsively. This impulsive behavior puts a dent on their leadership quality and their respect as a leader.

Emotional intelligence, in my view, is the most important and vital ingredient in the whole of the engaging leadership mix.

Lead By Engagement

Do you Know Yourself ?
Personality

The American Psychological Association (APA) defines personality as, "the individual differences in characteristic patterns of thinking, feeling and behaving. The study of personality focuses on two broad areas: One is understanding individual differences in particular personality characteristics, such as sociability or irritability. The other is understanding how the various parts of a person come together as a whole."

Personalities are characterized in terms of traits which are relatively enduring characteristics that influence our behavior across many situations. Personality traits such as introversion, friendliness, conscientiousness, honesty and helpfulness are important because they help explain consistencies in behavior.

The most popular way of measuring traits is by administering personality tests in which people are tasked to self-report about their own characteristics. Psychologists have investigated hundreds of traits using the self-report approach, and this research has found many personality traits that have important implications for behavior.

Lead By Engagement

It is very helpful to know your own personality and that of the people you work or live with. This helps in tailoring your approach and communication style to best suit another person you must work with.

Carl Jung

Carl Gustav Jung was a Swiss psychiatrist whose research was deep-rooted in psychoanalysis. He was greatly influenced by Sigmund Freud and even conducted research alongside this great icon. Eventually, though, Jung disagreed with many of Freud's theories. Jung is best known for his research in personality, dream analysis and the human psyche.

His theories are so revered that they were made into their own school of psychotherapy: Jungian psychology, also called analytical psychology. Let's look deeper into the main theories of Jungian psychology.

Personality Theory

In his theory of personality, Carl Jung distinguishes two different attitude types: introverts, those people who receive stimulation from within, and extroverts, those who receive their stimulation from the environment.

Introverts are generally more withdrawn, while extroverts are generally more sociable. For example, Jeanne is an extrovert. She loves to go out on adventures with lots of people and see exciting new things. Her friend Ahmed, though, is the opposite. Given the choice, he'd rather read a book on his couch than go skiing with Jeanne. Ahmed is an introvert.

Lead By Engagement

Jung also separates introverts and extroverts into four subtypes according to the functions that control the way they perceive the world. Both introverts and extroverts can be any of these subtypes, so there are eight possible personality types when you realize that each person is a mix of different levels with one or two being the dominate trait. These four functions are:

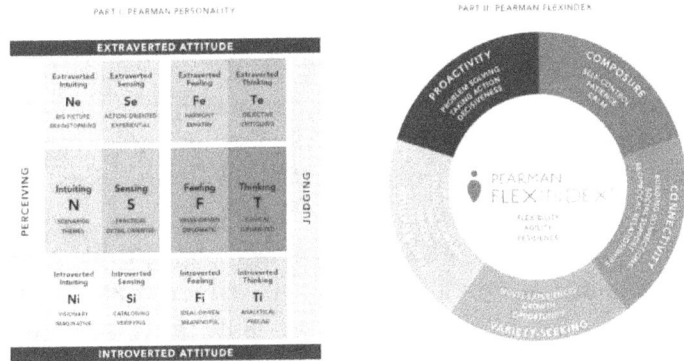

Pearman Personality Integrator Model

1. Thinking
Applying reasoning to the situations and environments you encounter. For example, Ahmed likes to think things through and consider all the pros and cons before he makes a decision about anything.

2. Feeling
Applying subjective, personal assessment to the situations and environments you encounter. Unlike Ahmed, Jeanne relies on her feelings to tell her how to make a decision. If something feels good, she goes for it; if it doesn't, she avoids it.

3. Sensation

Applying aesthetic value to the situations and environments you encounter. For example, when deciding how to arrange his living room, Ahmed tries to make things very symmetrical. If there's a picture on one side of the room, he has to put a similar picture on the other side of the room to balance it. This symmetry makes the room look nice to Ahmed.

4. Intuition

Using your unconscious or the mystical to understand your experiences. For example, Jeanne thinks Ahmed is decorating his room all wrong. She would rather use her intuition and put pictures and furniture asymmetrically.

Myer Briggs personality types and the Pearman Personality Integrator are also based on Carl Jung's personality theories. Pearman is unique in the sense that it does not believe in personality types or buckets. Dr. Roger Pearman believes that all humans are unique and it is not fair to put them in a bucket. As a matter of fact, I always believed that there was something missing in most personality theories. I felt that I was a different person in different environments or situations. Many people I worked with also felt unfulfilled working with types or buckets.

During those classic personality profiling tests one has to bucket people, this is how they work. However, the Pearman personality integrator is the most comprehensive and to me, nearest to reality. It measures three aspects of personality:

Lead By Engagement

1) Natural Personality
2) Demonstrated Personality
3) Flex Index

A natural personality is the personality you have developed over the years mixed partly with what you were born with. This remains constant most of your life. However, you are not given a type like D or A or ISFJ or ISTP. You are you, and you are unique.

The demonstrated personality is the personality that you demonstrate at different times. Most people work and live in an environment that is not in accordance with their natural personality and still thrive because they have a different personality activated in different circumstances.

The flex index is the measurement of the flexibility of the person to move from natural to demonstrated personality and vice versa. This shows the strength and flexibility a person has to work against one's natural personality and not break down easily.

I, personally, like the Pearman personality integrator the most. This gives me in depth analysis of my clients and their team members. I have been able to help my clients much better with this assessment in comparison with DiSC or MBTI.

If you know your personality in depth and that of your key direct reports, you will be able to engage them lot quicker and in a sustained manner. Knowing the personality of your key reports will also ensure that they are given the type of work and the environment that best suits their personality and they can be engaged with it.

Personality is fixed, it cannot really be changed in the short term. However, through some personality testing you will know the natural vs demonstrated

Lead By Engagement

personality of you and your team and also their flex index. This gives you a complete inside picture of the person and you can design an incentive plan and future plan of action, which will have much higher chance of success than without this detailed knowledge.

Lead By ENgagement

Increasing Employee Engagement

If employees truly are a company's best asset, then their care and support should be a priority.

Any employee engagement initiative must be a top down approach. The top management must push it down. However, engagement starts with each person and is subjective. If the employee engagement plan becomes a corporate priority, wonders can happen. If the corporations weave employee engagement as a performance expectation for all the managers, you will see results will go through the roof.

Most of the current practice managerial expectations are based on goal numbers. Sales, ROI, number of phone calls, number of complaints resolved, etc. The qualitative aspects of some goals are mentioned but are not given due importance or respect. This is a strategic step that top management has to take. If employee engagement becomes a top priority, the way all team leaders manage will shift to effective and ENGAGED leadership. As a result, employees will be more engaged, producing better and higher quality results.

Please refer to the Full Person Theory discussed earlier in this book. You also must remember that each person's potential extends well beyond their job

Lead By Engagement

description. Tapping that potential means recognizing how an employee's unique set of beliefs, talents, goals and life experiences drives their performance, personal success and well-being.

The actively disengaged employees are more or less out to damage your company. Not only are they unhappy at work, but they are intent on acting out their unhappiness. They monopolize managers' time and drive away customers. They annoy their coworkers, causing everyone around them to lose momentum and concentration. Whatever engaged employees do — such as solve problems, innovate and create new customers — actively disengaged employees will work to undermine. This type of employee is costing US corporations in excess of $300 billion each year. A severely disengaged employee will rarely be receptive to the work required in order to change, and therefore working with them is a waste of corporate time and resources.

However, an average employee who is just not engaged in their work offers perhaps the greatest untapped opportunity for businesses to improve their performance and profitability. Disengaged workers can be difficult to spot. They are not overtly hostile or disruptive and likely do just enough to fulfill their job requirements. They are uninspired and lacking in motivation. They have little or no concern about customers, productivity, profitability, safety or quality. They are thinking about lunch or their next break and have essentially checked out.

The majority of the global workforce is not engaged: most employees reluctantly head to work, lacking energy and passion for their jobs. Converting this group of employees into engaged workers is the

Lead By Engagement

most effective strategy that any organization can implement to increase performance and sustainable long-term growth.

If employees feel better about their jobs, they are less likely to leave. More important: they will try to be better at what they do.

A new employee joins your team excited, motivated and full of new ideas. Then as the days turn into months, the energy and enthusiasm they walked through the door with plateaus, then inevitably plummets.

For many organizations, keeping staff engaged is an ongoing struggle. If your people are disconnected and aren't engaged with the work they're doing, how can you expect potential customers to get excited about your company?

The negative impact of disengaged staff can also mean higher rates of absenteeism, lack of productivity, higher turnover, more room for human error, safety incidents and much more. Why does this happen? The number one reason for this is the people are not given the importance that they deserve. Human assets are not treated with the respect and care they need and do deserve. My observation is that many organizations do not regard people as their most important asset. This shows in their attitude and policies. People are smart, they know when they are not valued and so get back at the organization by just working enough to get by.

In many small businesses I have seen the owners regarding employees as mere tools to make money. If one does not fit in they are fired and a new one comes in. These types of owners are more worried about their machines and money then about their real asset — employees.

Lead By Engagement

I recommend a number of strategic steps organizations can take to remedy the situation. It needs a complete paradigm shift in the way management thinks.

Key Strategic Steps Are:

1) Make Employee Engagement a Corporate Priority
2) Create Positive Organizational Environment
3) Select Good Managers
4) Develop and Coach Managers
5) Weave employee engagement in manager performance expectations
6) Define engagement goals in realistic, everyday terms. To bring engagement to life
7) Know your employees well
8) Communicate well and often with employees
9) Engage employees in goal setting and planning. Share ownership of company objectives
10) Give employees what they need. Advance training, right tools and friendly environment
11) Act fairly and respectfully and create trust
12) Develop creative incentive programs
13) Develop and implement internal marketing initiatives

Lead By Engagement

In addition to these strategic steps and initiatives, some tactical steps can also be taken simultaneously to achieve employee engagement. We know that engagement is an individual issue, so it must be dealt with on an individual level.

It has been my experience that to employees the most important person in the office is their direct supervisor. This person can make a world of difference in the way employees think about their job and company. These managers can really make or break the engagement scene on an individual level.

Following are some tactical steps that I strongly recommend that managers should take to engage their employees. These can be taken by any size of organization. You understand your organization and with the EI and personality assessments and coaching, you now can sit down with each of your direct reports. Try to know them, understand their needs and ways of communication and implement as many of the steps you can based on your environment.

Lead By Engagement

Tactical Engagement Initiatives:

1) Know your employees
2) Communicate openly and often
3) Give and receive feedback regularly
4) Express gratitude
5) Spend time with employees
6) Start your day with a huddle
7) Be proactive about engagement
8) Tailor communication styles to employees
9) Involve employees in decision making
10) Help employees build dreams
11) Random fun activities
12) Help your team network
13) Positive reinforcement
14) Make the job meaningful
15) Make the small successes count
16) Help employees align dreams with company goals

Lead By Engagement

To complement group and individual recognition, it is strongly recommended to create a working environment that is rewarding just in itself. This encourages people to want to come to work and spend time with each other while also strengthening the loyalty they have to their team and company. This creates support for everyone in building a culture of spontaneity and fun.

Conclusion

Leading the way for your company and team is a great responsibility. You are the leader, it is your responsibility to lead by example and first get engaged with your employees and then lead them to engage their own teams.

Engaging a team is a company matter and it is also equally a personal matter. The implementation and real impact is on an individual level.

As a leader you have to know and do all or most of the things I discussed in this book. I will lay them down once again briefly as a summary:

- Engagement is to attract and hold interest. It is sustained employee motivation that comes from inside and outside.
- To have employees engaged, they must have their minds and hearts engaged and not just be punctual with low absenteeism.
- The first step in employee engagement is that the leaders and managers must be engaged with their employees and then *and only then* can they expect their employees to be engaged with work.
- Humans are a lot more than just their job description. No matter what the person does in the company, they are a full person. A full

Lead By Engagement

person is a lot more than a computer programmer or telephone operator or an HR specialist.
- All people are full persons. A combination of a physical body, brain and ideas, emotions and spirituality. All of these aspects must be catered to in order to motivate a person to be fully engaged.
- Leaders must know and understand themselves and their team members.
- Leaders must know their own and their employees' emotional intelligence level and personality.
- Emotional intelligence assessments can give leaders an in-depth look into their own areas of strengths and the ones they need to improve. Higher EI can help them develop highly engaged teams and reduce losses due to disengagement.
- Development of EI will make more effective leaders and workers. No matter what your role is or what your position is in an organization, higher EI will make you do things better and produce better results in comparison to low EI or just emotions or just intelligence.
- There are various personality theories and assessments developed by psychologists. Personality assessments also help tremendously in understanding yourself and your employees. This can give you answers to many unanswered questions. Use any of the assessments that work for you. I believe that Pearman personality test is the most comprehensive and effective assessment.
- There are a number of steps you can take as an organization or department head to improve

Lead By Engagement

engagement. These steps are both strategic and tactical in nature.
- Engagement is a corporate as well as a personal issue.
- Engagement must be endorsed as a priority by the top management, however, the implementation and actual impact must be made on a personal and individual level.
- An engaged employee is the one who has both mind and heart fully engaged.

About the Author

Moaz "Mo" Sharif is a Ziglar Legacy certified trainer. He is also an Emotional Intelligence EQ-i 2.0, EQ 360, DISC and Pearman Personality Integrator certified trainer and coach.

Empowering people and developing inspiring leaders is his passion. His training and coaching programs are designed to help people discover their hidden potential and then unleash it. His training is designed to dig one deeper and push forward. He believes in success by design and shares his personal experiences of both failures and successes so people can avoid the pitfalls and achieve success through teams. He has blended the Zig Ziglar's proven methodology with latest developments in Emotional Intelligence, Personality, Mindfulness and Thought Detoxing.

Lead By Engagement

In addition to holding an MBA degree, Sharif has over thirty years of global experience in leading teams, launching products and developing leaders, out of which about two decades are in USA and Canada.

In addition to this book Sharif has written several blogs and has a free YouTube Channel - MO for MOTIVATION.

Learn more by visiting www.transformcatalyst.com

Other books Moaz "Mo" Sharif is authoring:

-Change Your Habits and Rise: Fastest Way to Transformation is to Replace Your Bad Habits with Good Ones

-Ordinary Persons - Extraordinary Lives: There is Nothing Ordinary About Ordinary

TransformativeCatalyst

Lead By Engagement

www.ingramcontent.com/pod-product-compliance
Lightning Source LLC
Chambersburg PA
CBHW052334220526
45472CB00001B/420